S0-ACJ-418

This journal belongs to

shaunti feldhahn
and lisa a. rice

for young women only

discussion journal

MULTNOMAH
BOOKS

FOR YOUNG WOMEN ONLY DISCUSSION JOURNAL
PUBLISHED BY MULTNOMAH BOOKS
12265 Oracle Boulevard, Suite 200
Colorado Springs, Colorado 80921
A division of Random House Inc.

ISBN 978-1-60142-038-1

Library of Congress Cataloging-in-Publication Data
Feldhahn, Shaunti Christine.
    For young women only discussion journal / Shaunti Feldhahn and Lisa A. Rice. — 1st ed.
        p. cm.
    ISBN 978-1-60142-038-1
  1. Man-woman relationships—Religious aspects—Christianity. 2. Man-woman relationships.
3. Men—Psychology. 4. Marriage—Religious aspects—Christianity. 5. Marriage. I. Rice, Lisa Ann. II. Title.
    BT708.5.F453 2007
    248.8'33—dc22

                                    2007011394

Printed in the United States of America
2007—First Edition

10 9 8 7 6 5 4 3 2 1

To Sarah, Hannah, and Merry Beth—
three of the wisest teenagers we know.

Contents

A Word from the Authors

Be honest: what drew you to this discussion journal—or to the book *For Young Women Only*? Did it have anything to do with the hot guy on the cover?

If you just got busted on that question, you're not alone. Frankly, most girls are curious about what's going on in the minds of the guys they know— especially if the guys are cute. That's why we wrote *For Young Women Only* to begin with: so we females could better understand how guys think.

If you've read the book, you know it's packed with interesting comments straight from guys. You may have found yourself asking the guys around you, "Is this stuff true?" After hearing the fifth guy say, "Uh, yeah," you realized that you need to do a lot more thinking about what guys are really like...and what this means for *you*.

Ever since *For Young Women Only* came out, we've been receiving e-mails and letters from girls across the country saying, essentially, "I can't believe I didn't see these things before!" And many are asking, "How do I apply these truths to my life?"

That's exactly why we developed this companion discussion journal.

A Different Sort of Journal

Although this journal may look a little different than the ones you're used to, we think you'll find it a helpful and safe place to record your thoughts about guys, God, and life. We designed it to serve as a starting point for in-depth conversations with yourself, with your friends, and with God.

Each chapter, or conversation, corresponds to a chapter in the main book, which you'll want to read (or perhaps reread) along with this interactive companion journal. We include a summary of each chapter at the beginning, but we cannot communicate all the important ideas in a summary. So please take the time to familiarize yourself with the chapter before beginning the corresponding conversation in this journal.

You'll find key questions to think about and respond to in your own personal time, along with plenty of space to record your thoughts, prayers, questions, and hopes each day. Scattered throughout are helpful Bible verses, guidance for prayers, and other bits and pieces that may spark some new ideas you'll want to jot down.

We hope you'll also use this as an opportunity to connect with other girls and compare notes. Many are studying the book in their youth groups, school clubs, or with a small group of trusted friends. You can share your thoughts on what you've learned, what the guys in the book said, examples you've observed that confirm or contradict the survey results, and, of course, what it all means when it comes to real life.

Each chapter follows the same format, starting with pages for **you as an individual:**

- a Recap of the chapter.
- a place to Rethink your ideas, with questions based on what you've read.
- room to React to what others are saying.
- space to Reconsider your perspectives and plan healthy changes. (Yes, we know we've got the whole *R* thing going. Humor us…)
- lots of room to record your Reflections, Remembrances, and Random Thoughts—anything that comes to mind and everything you want to pray about.

The last part of every chapter—look for the shaded pages—contains three segments designed specifically for **group discussion:**

- questions and ideas for helping you Relate what you're learning in conversations with your small group or trusted friends.
- a Rewind and Replay case study featuring a true-to-life scenario designed to help you get inside the mind of a guy (scary, we know!) and put your new insights to work. (We've omitted this element from the first and last chapters to allow more personal journaling space.)
- a Real-Life Challenge that prompts you to apply what you're learning to your life and, if you want, report back to the group next time you meet.

Make It Work for You!

You can share as much or as little as you feel comfortable discussing with others. This is your journal, so make it work for you. While we believe you'll benefit from talking over the insights with trusted friends, we've designed this book so you can just open to the last few pages during group discussions and keep the rest private, if that's what you want.

And your group can follow whatever format makes the most sense, mixing and matching the elements to meet your unique goals. For example, one group might decide to meet for eight weeks or more, taking a week or two to cover each subject and going through each of the elements in detail. Another group may want to meet for a shorter period, combining chapters, and only tackling the Rethink and Relate questions for each topic. Or some groups may want to focus on the Rewind and Replay case studies and questions along with the Real-Life Challenges.

As you make your way through this journal, please keep in mind that *For Young Women Only* is not an equal treatment of male-female differences, nor does this guide delve into what guys need to understand about girls. (That's a whole different book, *For Young Men Only*, which we'll be publishing soon so the guys can learn more about you! Check out www.foryoungmenonly.com.)

However you choose to use this resource, we pray that God will open your eyes to things you may not have seen before. We encourage you to respond to God's invitation, offered thousands of years ago through the prophet Jeremiah: "Call to me and I will answer you and tell you great and unsearchable things you do not know" (33:3).

An exciting journey lies ahead, and we're eager to hear about each step of your adventure. Please visit our website at www.foryoungwomenonly.com, and send us your comments, suggestions, and other feedback as you go.

Blessings,

Shaunti and Lisa

WHAT IN THE WORLD ARE THESE GUYS THINKING?

The Question on Every Girl's Mind

Recap

Whether you're reading this book for fun, curiosity, or out of desperation, we believe you'll come away with a new perspective on how guys think that you can apply to your life.

In preparation for writing *For Young Women Only*, we interviewed and surveyed hundreds of guys across the country, and the following chart outlines six major findings most likely to affect your relationships. The column on the left, "Our Surface Understanding," is what we girls generally know about guys, and the column to the right, "What That Means in Practice," is a specific—and often surprising—revelation about how that general understanding plays out in everyday life.

Our Surface Understanding	What That Means in Practice
Guys need respect.	Guys would rather feel unloved than inadequate and disrespected.

Our Surface Understanding	What That Means in Practice
Guys are insecure.	Although guys look confident—even cocky at times—they are often insecure in themselves. They worry that they will be found out, and therefore are drawn to girls who help them feel like they measure up.
Guys are tough and indestructible.	Guys look indestructible, but on the inside their hearts are tender, easily hurt, and strongly guarded. However, they will let down their defenses when they know their heart will be safe with a girl.
Guys are visual.	Even decent guys in great dating relationships struggle with the desire to visually linger on and fantasize about the female body—and much of that struggle depends on what a girl is wearing.
Guys are all out for one thing.	Teenage guys are conflicted by their powerful physical desires, which also have massive emotional consequences. Guys need your help to protect both of you.
Guys go after the hot girls.	Guys are attracted to girls with a good personality as well as inner and outer beauty, but they can't force a physical attraction.

Each of the chapters to follow corresponds to one of these six major findings, helping you figure out what the findings mean for you. So brace yourself for some life-changing conversations with God, your friends, and yourself. But first, a sneak peek at the sort of thing you're going to read:

The loveliness and attractiveness of girls causes us
to excel—to want to be smarter, faster, and better at
everything—all to impress and win the girl. Remember,
everything—*everything*—is to impress chicks.
—teen guy quoted in FYWO, p. 98

Rethink

Which of the six major findings seems most surprising to you—even unlikely—and why?

The one I found different was the respect one that a guy would work so hard to get respect.

If you could ask a guy anything about guys—and be sure he'd answer honestly—what would you ask?

Can a guy like a girl and have a relationship without wanting to get phycil

What stereotypes in the media might contribute to girls' confusion about guys?

The media makes all guys look like physical is all they want and nothing else.

How do you feel about leaving behind your thoughts on how guys should be and coming to terms with the truth of who they are and what that means for you?

Im ok I have an open mind and Im ready for anything.

Proverbs 3:13–14 says, "Joyful is the person who finds wisdom, the one who gains understanding. For wisdom is more profitable than silver, and her wages are better than gold" (NLT). How can you be sure that whatever you read in this book is translated into true wisdom for living?

If its from the bible then I should be following it because gods word and direction is all I need.

React

His Perspective: "I'm glad that girls will finally be able to understand that we're not just all about food and sex—though that's pretty huge, I admit—but we really do have feelings and goals and can sometimes thoughtfully express ourselves about the opposite sex." —Jonathan, seventeen

Her Response: "It's nice to hear guys being vulnerable about their insecurities and girl fears and wiring systems. It makes them seem more real and less like the stereotypes we've seen and heard." —Sarah, seventeen

Your Insights: Why do you think guys don't just tell us these things directly? How might a reluctance to talk honestly with each other affect relationships? What dangers, if any, might there be in talking too openly?

I think guys feel like it they talk about their feelings then that will make them look weak.

Reconsider

When it comes to guys, I really don't understand…

Why so many are players and why they are willing to do stuff for me but never for themselfs.

One thing I know I need God's wisdom for is…

Every step Im making at this point in my life, with guys being not settling for less. And also with friends.

Reflections, Remembrances, and Random Thoughts

Sometimes I make dumb decisions and don't listen to god.

Here's what's on my mind this week, Father...

Come near to God and he will come near to you.
—James 4:8

Surely you desire truth in the inner parts; you teach me wisdom in the inmost place.

—Psalm 51:6

To Think About

How does God usually teach me wisdom?

Prayer for Today

Lord, help me to draw close to you and hear your voice about my life. Teach me how to view my future—especially the way I think about guys and dating. I know your plans for me are amazing.

Let patience have its perfect work, that you may be perfect and complete, lacking nothing.

—James 1:4 (NKJV)

To Think About

Where do I need to exercise patience?

Prayer for Today

Father, help me to see how you're using the circumstances in my life to change me for the better.

To Think About

Am I harboring bitterness over the pain someone has inflicted on my heart?

The glory of Christianity is to conquer by forgiveness.

—William Blake

Prayer for Today

Lord, teach me to forgive richly and fully, just as you have richly and fully forgiven me.

Oh, how I love your law!
I meditate on it all day long.

—Psalm 119:97

To Think About

Do I care as much about what God says as what others say? How much time do I spend in reading his Word and being in his presence?

Prayer for Today

Father, increase my shield of faith as I hear and apply your Word. I know that faith pleases you, and I want to please you with all my heart.

Keep true to the dreams of thy youth.

—Friedrich von Schiller

> ## To Think About
> What kind of guy do I hope to one day marry? And what kind of woman do I hope to become?

Delight yourself in the LORD and he will give you the desires of your heart.
—Psalm 37:4

God's Answers to Prayer This Week

> Faith and prayer are the vitamins of the soul; man cannot live in health without them.
>
> —Mahalia Jackson

Relate—What Are These Guys Thinking?

Talk with your small group or trusted friends about what you're hoping to gain (or have gained) from reading *For Young Women Only*. Look back through your journal entries from this past week, and write below anything you'd like to talk about.

_____

_____

_____

_____

_____

_____

_____

_____

_____

_____

_____

_____

_____

_____

_____

Here are a few ideas for launching into your discussion:

- What were your thoughts about the questions on pages 7–8?
- Do guys think about us as much as we think about them? What have you seen that supports your answer?
- Where do you usually get information about guys—parents, magazines, movies, other girls? What are the benefits and drawbacks of those sources?
- How can we make our discussion group a safe place for sharing our insights and struggles with one another?

Real-Life Challenge

Here are some action challenges for you this week:

- Look back over the chart with the six major findings. Which were you already aware of, and how are you applying them in your life?
- Which of these findings about how guys really work is the most likely to require changes in your life?

You can jot down notes about the outcome of this challenge on page 46. If you feel comfortable doing so, share your answers with your trusted friends or small group the next time you meet.

YOUR LOVE IS *NOT* ENOUGH

You Mean He Wants My Respect More Than My Love?

Recap
Guys would rather feel alone and unloved than inadequate and disrespected.

Were you surprised to discover that a guy's need for respect and affirmation—especially from the main girl in his life—is even more important than his need for love? Two out of three guys on the national survey agreed that they'd rather feel unloved than inadequate! And the importance of respect only increases over time. Three out of four adult men prefer respect over love.

Guys admitted that just about everything they do is meant to impress girls, so getting disrespect from those girls is especially devastating.

> I'd rather be alone and unloved. For a guy, being disrespected is just not right. *I'd rather be by myself than have someone disrespect me.*
> —teen guy quoted in FYWO, p. 22

Rethink

What surprised you most in this chapter?

Think of a time you communicated disrespect to a guy, even if you didn't mean to. If you had another chance, what would you do differently, based on what you've learned?

Now think of a time you got it right, and describe how you knew that the guy appreciated your respect.

Do the guys you're closest to tend to let you know when they're feeling disrespected? If they don't express it out loud, how do they communicate their frustration?

Ephesians 5:33 says, "Each one of you also must love his wife as he loves himself, and the wife must respect her husband." How might the relationship habits you're building now affect your marriage later?

React

His Perspective: "Guys do need to feel like they're an expert at something. The movie *Napoleon Dynamite* even jokes about girls liking guys with skills. 'You know, like nun-chuck skills, bow hunting skills, computer hacking skills....' If a guy has skills, and a girl doesn't consider it important, he feels totally belittled and disrespected. Every guy is trying to gather a collection of skills so he'll feel tops at something. And if a girl doesn't trust him in *that* area—which he does know something about—he's going to question whether she could trust him in *any* area." —quote from a guy-on-the-street interview

Her Response: "I couldn't believe it when I read the whole respect thing in your book. I had no idea guys were more respect-based than love-based. I've been treating guys like girls in that way, but hopefully those days are over." —e-mail from a teenage girl

Your Insights: What have you learned about yourself and the guys in your life from this chapter? How might your new insights affect your behavior in the future?

Reconsider

Here's where I struggle when it comes to showing guys respect:

One change I plan to make because of what I've learned is...

Reflections, Remembrances, and Random Thoughts

Here's what's on my mind this week, Father...

Your Father knows what you need before you ask him.
—*Matthew 6:8*

Two out of three guys agreed that they'd prefer to be unloved—just don't make them feel inadequate!

—FYWO, p. 21

To Think About

When today might
my words have
wounded someone?

Prayer for Today

*What would you like to change in me, Lord? I know you
always want what's best for me, and I want to please you.*

Crying is often a woman's response to feeling unloved, and anger is often a man's response to feeling disrespected.

—Dr. Emerson Eggerichs, quoted in FYWO, p. 26

To Think About

Have I seen any unexplained anger from guys that might have been sparked by my being disrespectful without realizing it?

Prayer for Today

Lord, teach me to be sensitive to my family and friends.
Help me not to provoke others to anger, but to walk in kindness.

To Think About

Have my conversations today reflected respect in both tone and words?

No change of circumstances can repair a defect of character.

—Ralph Waldo Emerson

Prayer for Today

Lord, teach me the heart attitudes you want me to learn while I'm still young.

Guys have a built-in desire to save the damsel in distress.... We'll change your flat in a blinding snowstorm, and we'll carry furniture upstairs in 95 percent humidity if you ask nicely.... But if she doesn't act grateful and respectful, we've lost our motivation.

—teen guy quoted in FYWO, p. 34

To Think About

Do I do a good job of affirming and appreciating those who do things for me? Guy friends? Girl friends? Siblings?

Prayer for Today

Lord, work in my heart and life today, continuing the process of transforming me into the woman you created me to be.

Prayer is keeping
company with God.
—Clement of Alexandria

> ### To Think About
>
> Do I spend as much time listening to the opinions of others as I do expressing my own thoughts? What about my prayer time? Am I listening to God or focusing on what I want from him?

But I, by your great mercy, will come into your house;
in reverence will I bow down toward your holy temple.
—Psalm 5:7

God's Answers to Prayer This Week

Prayer is the key that opens to us the treasures of God's mercies and blessings.

—Henry Ward Beecher

Report on Last Week's Real-Life Challenge

Each time you meet, if you feel comfortable doing so, talk about how you did over the last few days on the previous Real-Life Challenge action items.

As I looked at the six major findings from *For Young Women Only,* here are the ones I already knew about and this is how that has affected my interactions with guys:

_____

_____

_____

_____

_____

This is the one surprise that will probably prompt the most changes in how I relate to guys:

_____

_____

_____

_____

_____

And here's what I'm going to do about it:

_____

_____

_____

_____

_____

Relate—Your Love Is Not Enough

Talk with your trusted friends, and compare notes on what you learned this week. Look back through your journal entries from this week, and write here a few things you'd like to discuss regarding guys and respect.

Here are a few more thoughts to get the conversational ball rolling:
- What were your thoughts about the questions on pages 28–29?
- In what circumstances do you most often tend to treat a guy with disrespect? Why do you think that is?
- What's the difference between speaking with respect and just laying on the flattery?
- How can we hold one another accountable for making respect the habit of our conversations and attitudes?

Rewind and Replay

Allison sat beside her boyfriend on the bus as they headed to the mountains for a youth-group ski trip. Although Greg put in a lot of hours at his family's pizza restaurant and worked other summer jobs to make ends meet, he and Allison had enjoyed finding time for fun outdoor activities while they'd been going out over the past several months. Today, however, Allison was nervous. Greg had been skiing dozens of times, but this was her first attempt, and she didn't want to look like a fool in front of her athletic guy. He'd made a couple of comments about wanting to teach her to ski, and during the long bus ride he gave her some tips. But those lessons her dad had mentioned still seemed like a pretty good idea.

When they arrived, Allison hustled over to the ski instruction area and snapped up the last spot in the morning class. Then she ran back to where Greg stood holding the brand-new skis she'd bought for the occasion, an expensive splurge, but her dad could afford it. "Guess what!" she announced. "My dad gave me some money for lessons, and they had one more space left, so I took it, okay? I'll see you back at the lodge for lunch." As she gave Greg a quick kiss, she noticed his expression tighten in a way that indicated he was upset. Not wanting to be late for the class, she hurried off. When she looked back, she saw him turn toward a ski lift with one of his buddies, who was shaking his head sympathetically. She started to feel a little irritated herself. This was supposed to be a fun day! What was his problem?

1. Why did Allison decide to get a private instructor? Would you have done the same? Why or why not?
2. Now put yourself in Greg's shoes. As he rode to the ski resort with Allison, what might he have been thinking the day would be like? What clues in their conversation indicate what he expected to happen?

3. How do you think he felt as he watched Allison sign up for private lessons, then hurry away? What messages was she unintentionally sending?
4. How might he describe Allison's opinion of him, not just in skiing but in other areas as well?
5. What difference might it have made to Greg that one of his friends was aware of what happened? Explain your answer.
6. If Allison could press a do-over button, would Greg deserve a different response from her? If so, what would that look like?

Note: After you think over these questions, check out the Inside His Head section at the end of this book to see what Greg was actually thinking.

Real-Life Challenge

Here are some action challenges for you this week:

- Observe the guys in your life and try to spot three situations where they might be feeling disrespected.
- Find three ways to show genuine respect to the guys you care about and briefly describe what happened.

You can jot down notes about the outcome of this challenge on page 70 and share the outcome with your friends the next time you meet.

Conversation 3

THE PERFORMANCE OF A LIFETIME

Mr. Gorgeous and Cocky Is Actually Insecure?

Recap

Although guys look confident, they are often insecure in themselves, worry that they will be found out, and are therefore drawn to girls who help them feel like they measure up.

Can you believe that so many of the guys strutting around your school are actually hiding a deep insecurity? Our survey revealed that many fear having their inadequacy exposed—even if they're perfectly capable of doing whatever it is they're feeling insecure about. To mask their insecurity, they do whatever it takes to look confident, often resorting to bravado, humor, or just plain faking it.

Guys are always on the lookout for signals that feed either their confidence or their insecurity. In particular, 77 percent of guys say they want the girls in their lives to help them feel that they measure up. A guy's secret insecurity is especially triggered when a girl nags or overquestions him, but he feels great when a girl compliments and verbalizes the good she sees in him. Encouraging words have tremendous power to bring to life the superhero in every male.

We think about what others think about us *all the time.*
—teen guy quoted in FYWO, p. 45

Rethink

As you read this chapter, what shifted in your thinking about the opposite sex?

Describe an occasion when you suspect that you unintentionally made a guy feel insecure.

Now give an example of a time you were able to affirm a guy and feed his confidence. How did he respond short term? long term?

What similarities do you see between guys and girls in feeling secretly insecure? What differences have you seen in how they tend to respond to those feelings?

How does your opinion of a guy change when you see that he doubts himself or is insecure? How do you think he feels about that?

In Colossians 3:12 we read, "As God's chosen people, holy and dearly loved, clothe yourselves with compassion, kindness, humility, gentleness and patience." In what ways might your interactions with guys change if you followed these instructions?

React

His Perspective: "A guy will go out of his way to avoid looking bad in physical activities. If he even suspects that a girl will be better, he usually won't participate. And guys really don't know how to handle the super-trash-talk stuff from a girl. They may laugh along now and avoid her later. If a girl is intellectually and athletically superior, even if she's totally hot, few guys will go after her unless they're super secure. That said, if she doesn't rub it in his face, it won't sting as bad and he might risk hanging out with her and doing stuff together. As guys mature, they realize that a girl's assets are actually a win-win for them, but we still like to be the knight in shining armor in some area." —quote from a guy-on-the-street interview

Her Response: "I couldn't believe I was doing all the things the book said not to. I was ragging on guys and teasing them and saying all kinds of things that now I'm sure they were wincing at. I finally realized why no guy would ever talk to me for more than three minutes. Yesterday, I tried being affirming instead, and ended up talking to one of the 'three-minute' guys on the phone for an hour!" —Melissa, high-school junior

Your Insights: What about you? How often do the comments you make in fun end up insulting others? As you read the perspective of a guy who wants to be a knight in shining armor, what response did that spark in you?

Reconsider

Here's where I tend to go wrong when it comes to building up a guy's confidence:

One change I plan to make because of what I've learned is…

Reflections, Remembrances, and Random Thoughts

Here's what's on my mind this week, Father...

We know that in all things God works for the good of those who love him, who have been called according to his purpose.
—Romans 8:28

Guys do pretend sometimes, hoping we're right. We take guesses and make it appear we know what we're doing...hoping we can figure it out later!

—teen guy quoted
in FYWO, p. 42

To Think About

What can I do to build up the confidence of the guys I care about?

Prayer for Today

Father, help me not to increase the insecurities of others, but to be an encourager.

It's good when a girl makes you feel you measure up. It's the opposite of disrespect, which I hate. It makes you feel you're worth something, that you have what it takes, that she likes you and believes in you.

—teen guy quoted
in FYWO, p 56

To Think About

How have my recent words or actions made others feel valued?

Prayer for Today

Let the words of my mouth and the meditation of my heart be acceptable in Your sight, O LORD, my strength and my Redeemer.
—*Psalm 19:14 (NKJV)*

To Think About

How can I be used by God
to bring out the best in
those around me?

> Let us consider how we may spur one another on toward love and good deeds.
>
> —Hebrews 10:24

Prayer for Today

Lord, teach me to follow the Golden Rule and to live with an unselfish, others-focused attitude every day.

It speaks volumes when a girl chooses to look at the good in me, even when she's upset. Part of respect is looking past the stupid circumstances and saying, "How can we work this out?" My girlfriend's unselfishness in that way makes me want to be a better man. She makes me want to step up to the plate.

—teen guy quoted in FYWO, p. 59

For out of the over-
flow of the heart the
mouth speaks.

—Matthew 12:34

Prayer for Today

*Lord, thank you for continually shaping me into
the image of Jesus. Please let the words I speak
reflect your grace-filled presence in my life.*

My girlfriend is always out for my best interest. She gives me heartfelt friendship and support. She has no problem giving me a slap in the face, but it's okay be-cause *I know she's always acting in my best interest.*

—teen guy quoted
in FYWO, p. 59

To Think About

What message am I giving the guys I care about? Do my words, tones, or actions imply, "You're not quite good enough"? Or do they suggest, "Go get 'em, tiger!"?

We will speak the truth in love, growing in every way more and more like Christ.
—Ephesians 4:15 (NLT)

God's Answers to Prayer This Week

Pray as though everything depended on God; work as though everything depended on you.

—Augustine of Hippo

Report on Last Week's Real-Life Challenge

Here are the three situations this past week where I noticed a guy might be feeling disrespected:

1 _____

2 _____

3 _____

These are the three ways I showed genuine respect to the guys I care about, and what happened:

1 _____

2 _____

3 _____

Relate—Performance of a Lifetime

Talk with your trusted friends, and compare notes on what you learned this week. Look back through your journal entries from this week, and write here a few things you'd like to discuss about helping guys overcome their hidden insecurities.

Here are a few things you may want to talk about:
- What were your thoughts about the questions on pages 52–53?
- What are the most obvious signals that a guy is feeling insecure? What are some other, more subtle signals we can watch for?
- Where do we draw the line between playful teasing and potentially hurtful comments?
- Do we have to hide our own strengths to avoid making guys feel inferior? If not, how can we build guys up without being untrue to ourselves?

Rewind and Replay

Hannah had recently moved to town and decided to shoot some hoops at the little neighborhood basketball court. She was delighted when a cute guy ran up and stole the ball. He introduced himself as Tyler. "How 'bout a quick game of one-on-one?" he baited, swishing the ball into the basket with ease. "Sure," Hannah replied, grinning. "But prepare to lose." Sure enough, she trounced him. She wondered if she should mention that she was the new center of the JV basketball team, but didn't get around to it. Tyler laughed when she won and vowed to show his true skills another time; right now he had to get home for dinner.

The following Monday, the first day of school, Hannah was thrilled to find Tyler sitting a few desks over in her algebra class. As the new students introduced themselves, Tyler mentioned that he knew Hannah from the neighborhood and that they'd shot hoops together. Before he could finish his sentence, Hannah blurted out, "Tell 'em who smoked who!" The whole class laughed, and Tyler did too. He cracked a joke about how gentlemen always let the girl win, and everyone laughed again.

Hannah was excited to have found a cool guy friend who liked basketball and had a great sense of humor, and she looked forward to playing lots of one-on-one in the neighborhood. The thing is, it didn't happen. Tyler never mentioned basketball again, and he rarely talked to her in algebra. "I'll never understand guys," she said, sighing, to her girlfriends.

1. Put yourself in Tyler's shoes. How do you think he was feeling before the one-on-one game? after the one-on-one game?
2. How might he have been feeling when he saw Hannah walk into the algebra class? What did his words seem to indicate about his interest in her?

3. How might her retort to the class have made him feel? What change might her words have prompted in his feelings toward her?
4. What secret feeling inside Tyler was triggered by Hannah's actions and words?
5. What, if anything, did Hannah do wrong? Was Tyler being too sensitive?
6. Describe how Hannah could have handled the situation to bring about a different response.

Note: After you think over these questions, check out the Inside His Head section at the end of this book to see what Tyler was actually thinking.

Real-Life Challenge

Here are some action challenges for you this week:

- Observe the guys in your life and try to spot at least three areas where they might be feeling insecure. What clues can you find to indicate how they're really feeling, and how do they try to cover it up?
- If you catch yourself stepping on a guy's toes in this area, try to find a creative alternative to your usual response.

You can jot down notes about the outcome of this challenge on page 94 and talk over the results next time you meet.

TOUGH OR TENDER?

A Peek into the Real Heart of Mr. Tough Guy

Recap

Guys may look indestructible, but their hearts are tender, easily hurt, and strongly guarded. Yet they will let down their defenses when they know their heart is safe with you.

Despite that seemingly tough exterior, guys are actually tender and easily hurt on the inside. But they don't want to risk showing their real emotions. In fact, 86 percent of guys said that they withhold their inner feelings from girls. Two-thirds of those guys said it's because they don't trust girls to handle their personal information with care. As one guy said, "Vulnerability is a four-letter word."

Many guys say they don't trust girls to be safe because they see how girls treat each other. They see lots of gossip and ruthlessness, just like in the movie *Mean Girls*. No way do they want to risk getting emotionally close and becoming a girl's next victim. Guys say the things they hate most are negative judgments, arguments, deception, gossip, jealousy, and especially meanness.

The good news is that all the guys surveyed said they know and admire many "safe" girls, good friends who listen, understand, and affirm them when they do open up.

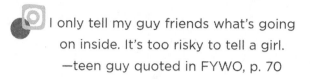 I only tell my guy friends what's going on inside. It's too risky to tell a girl.
—teen guy quoted in FYWO, p. 70

Rethink
What surprised you most in this chapter?

Are girls really as mean as guys seem to think? Explain your answer.

Describe a time when a guy witnessed you being gossipy or mean. What effect—whether seen or unseen—could that have had on your relationship?

Do the guys around you say anything outright to indicate that they believe you or another girl can't be trusted with their information or emotions? Or do they show it in another way?

We read in 1 Timothy 4:12, "Don't let anyone look down on you because you are young, but set an example for the believers in speech, in life, in love, in faith and in purity." What changes would take place in your life if you followed this advice in your relationships?

React

His Perspective: "Guys watch how you girls treat each other and think, *Is this girl going to hurt me like she hurt her friend? Am I the next fool?* I once told a girl my deepest emotions, and she broadcast them to everyone. I swore I would never do that again. You've gotta tell the girls that it's a lose-lose situation to be catty, because guys won't risk or hold their hearts out again." —quote from a guy-on-the-street interview

Her Response: "You nailed me on the mean-girls thing. My friends and I say so many nasty things to each other. Ninety percent of the time we're kidding around, but other people can't tell that, and truthfully, sometimes we can't either. I guess guys do see that and want to run." —e-mail from a high-school reader of FYWO

Your Insights: What do you think? Were you surprised that guys notice and care how you treat other girls? What about their concerns that you'll burn them if they risk being open with you? What light does this shed on any past relationship problems?

Reconsider
My mouth gets me into trouble when I…

One change I plan to make because of what I've learned is…

Reflections, Remembrances, and Random Thoughts

Here's what's on my mind this week, Father...

The LORD is good, a refuge in times of trouble.
—Nahum 1:7

We heard story after story about how parents, teachers, and peers have "burned" the guys they care about through careless words or actions.

But especially devastating was the pain of being hurt by girls.

—FYWO, p. 71

To Think About

If I'm honest with myself, have I sometimes failed to handle others' personal information with care?

Prayer for Today

Lord, I want to become a trustworthy friend to those you've placed in my life, and I ask you to be the gatekeeper of all my friendships.

[Some] girls will seduce, connive, deceive, manipulate, split, divide and conquer—all types of control—to make sure they will never be hurt again.

—counselors Clay and Cheryl Kull, FYWO, p. 73

To Think About

In what ways have I seen people be unpleasant to others to avoid being hurt themselves? When have I done this myself?

Prayer for Today

Dear Lord, please forgive me for manipulating circumstances to meet my own needs. Forgive me for seeking approval and power through manipulation instead of trusting you. I choose to trust you now with all my relationships.

To Think About

How could I be "safe"
for a guy to trust me
with his heart?

It comes down to the Golden Rule: "Do unto others as you would have them do unto you." Do you want a friend? Then be a friend. Do you want a safe place for your secrets? Then be a secret-keeper. Do you want to be built up and affirmed? Then do the same for those you care about. We promise—it'll all come back to you in the end.

—FYWO, p. 84

Prayer for Today

Father, I pray that you will purify my heart. Let my words and actions bring life and joy to those who fear rejection.

Some cause happiness wherever they go; others, whenever they go.

—Oscar Wilde

To Think About

In what circumstances do I tend to talk without thinking about how my words affect others?

Prayer for Today

*Father, let my words be few, wise, and thoughtful.
May I represent your name and your heart to others
in a way that pleases you and benefits those you love.*

I have often regretted my speech, never my silence.

—Xenocrates

To Think About

If I could go back through this day, how would I change the words I've spoken?

For wisdom will enter your heart, and knowledge will be pleasant to your soul. Discretion will protect you, and understanding will guard you.
—Proverbs 2:10–11

God's Answers to Prayer This Week

Prayer requires
more of the heart
than of the tongue.

—Adam Clarke

Report on Last Week's
Real-Life Challenge

Here are the three situations where I noticed a guy might be feeling insecure and the clues that gave it away:

1 _____
_____
_____

2 _____
_____
_____

3 _____

Some of the ways guys seemed to be covering their insecurities:

_____
_____
_____
_____
_____
_____
_____

When I realized a guy was feeling insecure, here's the creative idea I tried for building up his confidence:

_____
_____
_____
_____
_____
_____
_____

Relate—Tough or Tender?

Talk with your trusted friends, and compare notes on what you learned this week. Look back through your journal entries from this week, and write here a few things you'd like to discuss regarding what guys want in a girl and what it means to be a safe friend.

Here are a few questions you may want to discuss:
- What were your thoughts about the questions on pages 76–77?
- Why is the way girls talk such a huge deal for guys? Is it because they don't understand how we work?
- What kind of behaviors might look like meanness to guys? What's really behind those words and actions?
- How will we act differently now that we know how guys feel?
- How can we hold one another accountable to speak in ways that make others feel safe?

Rewind and Replay

Jen was amazed by "Rawhide Rick," as his teammates called him. A running back, he was constantly tackled, grabbed, pushed, and even stomped on when the refs weren't watching. But being abused, bruised, and battered never seemed to bother him; he just got up to keep playing—and scoring.

After each game, Jen and some other cheerleaders went out with the athletes for pizza. She was giddy when Rick sat near her and offered several times to drive her home. Hoping he'd ask her to homecoming, she never missed an opportunity to flirt with him, teasing Rick about everything from his sports injuries and his old car to his struggles in geometry and bad timing with jokes. She also kept the conversation rolling by filling him in on the happenings at school—who was seeing whom, who was breaking up with whom, and whatever else was going on under the surface. Jen enjoyed having the inside scoop, and sharing her knowledge was a surefire way of developing a closer relationship with Rick.

One Friday night over pizza, Jen told a funny story about an embarrassing incident that happened to Suzy, another cheerleader who hadn't joined them this time. Rick grew noticeably quiet, and he didn't offer to drive her home. What was up with that? For a moment, Jen wondered if maybe Rick liked Suzy. But how could he? She was way too quiet and had none of the spunk that guys obviously loved. And she never had good stories to tell! Jen would just have to turn up the charm so Rick wouldn't ask the wrong girl to the dance.

1. In Jen's mind, what were her own strengths and weaknesses?
2. Now put yourself in Rick's shoes. How might he have felt about Jen's teasing?
3. Keep yourself in Rick's shoes. How might he have felt about Jen's talking about others?

4. Why do you think Rick got so quiet on that particular Friday night?
5. In what ways might Jen have misjudged herself and others?
6. What, if anything, could Jen change at this point to convince Rick that she's the girl for him?

Note: After you think over these questions, check out the Inside His Head section at the end of this book to see what Rick was actually thinking.

Real-Life Challenge

Here are some action challenges for you this week:

- Observe the guys and girls around you this week. Which group seems to be safer with each other's personal information, and why do you think that is?
- If you catch yourself being an unsafe friend, or even a mean girl, stop, apologize, and try to start over with a clean slate. Notice the effect on your relationships when you're careful with your words.

You can jot down notes about the outcome of this challenge on page 118 to discuss next time you meet.

KEEPER OF THE PHOTO FILES

What "Guys Are Visual" Really Means...and What It Means for You

Recap

Even decent guys in great dating relationships struggle with a desire to visually linger on and fantasize about the female body—and much of that struggle depends on what a girl is wearing.

Those minutes you linger in the closet trying to decide what to wear really do matter. An outfit that calls attention to your figure can make you an eye magnet that, according to most guys, is incredibly difficult to avoid. And every guy has a mental photo album of images that can pop into his thoughts without warning or be called up at will.

The problem is, this admiration is not the sort a girl wants. When a guy checks you out, your brain may say, "He thinks I'm cute"—but as one guy noted, "*Cute* is not in a guy's vocabulary." Instead, when a guy sees (or recalls) a girl whose outfit draws attention to her figure, he's strongly tempted to picture her naked—or even naked with him.

Though it's not a sin to be drawn to eye magnets, those visual images stimulate some powerful feelings in guys that left unchecked can lead to sin. And although all young men bear responsibility for how they respond to temptation, why would we, if we truly care about them, want to contribute to their struggle?

Since we now know that our clothing choices—yes, even our favorite spaghetti-strap tops—may trigger images that hurt the guys we care about, let's consider what changes we can make that will honor their efforts to be pure.

> When we see a hot girl, the first ten seconds of a guy's thoughts are pretty raw. We go straight into the fantasy mode. And we have to really work to pull things back.
> —teen guy quoted in FYWO, p. 97

Rethink

What in this chapter most challenged your thinking about guys, or was most helpful?

What evidence have you seen that guys are indeed tempted visually in the ways described in this chapter?

If your clothing is a sign that sends a message to guys, what message is being sent by some of the items in your wardrobe?

Think about the guy you hope to one day marry. What do you hope he'll find most attractive about you?

If you could talk honestly with the girls who are now hanging out with your future husband, how would you ask them to dress and behave, and what reasons would you give them?

What ideas do the following verses give you for being an attractive young woman, and how might they apply in the modern day? "Your beauty should not come from outward adornment, such as braided hair and the wearing of gold jewelry and fine clothes. Instead, it should be that of your inner self, the unfading beauty of a gentle and quiet spirit, which is of great worth in God's sight" (1 Peter 3:3–4).

React

His Perspective: "Girls, if you want to help a guy out, learn to blend your inner beauty with your outer beauty. We know you have assets, and that's hard enough on our imaginations. You don't actually have to show them, outline them, glitterize them, or skintight them. We already know they're there, and that you're beautiful. Please put yourself in our shoes once in a while and realize that as we're working to pull these thoughts down, we could sure use your help. On behalf of all guys, I thank you." —e-mail from a guy reader of FYWO

Her Response: "It really creeped me out to read that guys might be picturing me naked. I guess I'm in that group that was totally clueless about how their brains are wired. As soon as I read it, I put on a less-tight shirt—fast!" —comment from a teenage girl after reading FYWO

Your Insights: Why are we so tempted to "glitterize" our assets, even after we know we're causing guys to struggle visually? Is it possible to dress in a way that makes you feel pretty but doesn't draw the wrong kind of attention? If so, what would that look like?

Reconsider

Here's the biggest challenge I see when it comes to dressing in a way that won't trigger temptation for guys around me:

Now that I realize how vulnerable guys are to visual stimulation, here's how that will affect my choices:

Reflections, Remembrances, and Random Thoughts

Here's what's on my mind this week, Father...

Call to Me, and I will answer you, and show you great
and mighty things, which you do not know.
—Jeremiah 33:3 (NKJV)

When I see that girl in the short skirt...I have to *force* myself to look away.... I'll think about cars, math, sports—whatever it takes to get my thoughts off that body.

—teen guy quoted in FYWO, p. 103

To Think About

Have I been honoring the guys around me by how I dress? Or could I have been making their struggles worse?

Prayer for Today

Father, please reveal to me any ways I'm making it more difficult for the guys in my life to resist temptation.

If you ever find yourself thinking, *It's no one's business what I wear,* or, *It's the guys' problem and they just have to get over it,* please realize that what you are actually saying is, *I want to do what I like, even if it hurts someone else.*

—FYWO, p. 111

To Think About

What responsibility do I have to help the guys around me keep their thoughts pure?

Prayer for Today

Lord, please establish my character while I am still young, and help me to set a godly example for those younger and older than me.

To Think About

By the clothes I wear and the way I carry myself, do I send the message "lure" or "pure"?

> A beautiful woman who lacks discretion is like a gold ring in a pig's snout.
>
> —Proverbs 11:22 (NLT)

Prayer for Today

Father, give me the gift of modesty so that your true beauty might shine through me without distraction.

Treat the guys you know like you would want the girls in your future husband's class to treat him! And we know that God will see to it that every good choice you make bears fruit. He'll always reward a heart that wants to do right.

—FYWO, p. 116

To Think About

How would I want the girls around my future husband to be treating him today? Are there any lessons in there for how I treat the guys around me?

Prayer for Today

Father, wherever my future husband is now, please bless him and keep him from the temptations that must constantly assault his mind.

Yes, you have to shop harder and longer to make modest choices, but when you do, you'll find that your self-worth rises...and you'll get the right kind of attention from the right kind of people.

—Vicki Courtney, FYWO, p. 115

Dress shabbily and they remember the dress; dress impeccably and they remember the woman.

—Coco Chanel

To Think About ✳

What kind of attention do I really want to attract? And what kind of guys do I hope will be interested in me?

Dress modestly, with decency and propriety, not with braided hair or gold or pearls or expensive clothes, but with good deeds, appropriate for women who profess to worship God.
—1 Timothy 2:9–10

God's Answers to Prayer This Week

Is prayer your steering wheel or your spare tire?

—Corrie ten Boom

Report on Last Week's Real-Life Challenge

Here's what I noticed about the differences between girls and guys and how they handle personal information:

_____

_____

_____

_____

_____

_____

Here's what happened when I caught myself being careless with someone else's information or starting to speak unkindly—and how things changed when I tried instead to be careful:

_____

_____

_____

_____

_____

Relate—Keeper of the Photo Files

Talk with your trusted friends, and compare notes on what you learned this week. Look back through your journal entries from this week, and write here a few things you'd like to discuss regarding the visual nature of guys.

_____

_____

_____

Here are a few discussion ideas you may want to cover:

- What were your thoughts about the questions on pages 100–102?
- Why does it matter what guys think about us?
- How would it make you feel to know that the guy you like is interested in you only for your body?
- If we don't wear clothes that show off our curves, how can we still be attractive and stylish?

Rewind and Replay

When Vicki's hopelessly flat chest finally started to develop, she was secretly delighted that she had a better figure than most of her friends. By the time summer came, she couldn't wait to get into a cute little bikini at the lake with her friends and post a picture on MySpace. She especially hoped James would appreciate it. They'd been in youth group together for years, and she'd dreamed that their friendship would one day grow into something more. Now she finally felt like she might grab his attention.

But instead of deepening into romance through the summer, their friendship seemed to lose its spark. What was up with James? He didn't come to the lake nearly as often as he used to. And was it her imagination, or did he suddenly look away whenever she came out of the water? It almost seemed like he was embarrassed. What had happened to their comfortable, carefree relationship? Maybe she'd ask him about it when they chatted online.

1. What prompted Vicki's eagerness to wear a bikini?
2. Put yourself in James's shoes. What, if anything, do you suppose was bothering him? Why was he acting so weird?
3. In what ways do you think James's opinion of his longtime friend might have changed since the start of summer and why?
4. How was Vicki potentially creating problems for their friendship?
5. If you were friends with her, what advice would you offer?
6. Do you think James would tell Vicki the truth if she questioned him online? Why or why not?

Note: After you think over these questions, check out the Inside His Head section at the end of this book to see what James was actually thinking.

Real-Life Challenge

Here are some action challenges for you this week:

- As you go about your day, watch for images that could be eye magnets if you were a guy. Make a mental note of what percentage of females on television or in public might pose a challenge for a guy who wants to have a clean thought life. Similarly, note examples of girls and women who dress attractively but without the "lure."
- Evaluate your own life to see if your wardrobe and/or attitudes are helping or hurting the guys you care about.

You can jot down notes about the outcome of this challenge on page 140.

SEEING THE INNER AND OUTER BEAUTY

Why Guys Care That Girls Take Care of Themselves...Even Though They Are Looking for the Real You

Recap

Guys are attracted to girls with good personalities, as well as inner and outer beauty and confidence. They want a real girl, not a perfect Barbie doll. But they can't force themselves to be attracted to someone.

Guys say they're much more interested in finding a "real" girl with a great personality than with finding a girl who's beautiful to look at but unpleasant to be with. However, three out of four say there does have to be physical attraction in order for them to be interested in dating a girl.

This is a hard topic to write about, since all of us—whether thin, pretty, overweight, small chested, or stocky—have some form of body insecurity that we already worry way too much about. The good news is that despite what we girls have trained ourselves to think, guys aren't looking for the *Sports Illustrated* swimsuit model. Nine out of ten say they're attracted to all different body and personality types.

Now, most do want girls to be a healthy weight (truly doctor-approved healthy, not Hollywood's emaciated ideal) and to make efforts on their appearance. Guys say a girl who's significantly overweight or disheveled, or a girl who wears skintight, inappropriate clothes, sends the signal that she doesn't feel very good about herself. Dr. Linda Mintle, a body-image psychotherapist, says that a girl can understand the guy's reaction by asking herself this question: *If I don't have enough respect for myself to want to take care of my body, why would a guy be eager to pursue knowing me better?* What we look like on the outside can reflect what's in our hearts, and when we're not taking care of ourselves, we send the message, *I don't care about myself.*

But don't just start trying to look good for a guy; that has its own problems! Dr. Mintle cautions that losing weight or making changes to how you present yourself in order to please a guy is a dangerous road. "Getting healthy should be motivated by wanting to take care of your body as the temple of the Holy Spirit and giving the message that you respect yourself, regardless of the opinions of others." Since many women—even thin ones—tend to think they need to lose weight, Dr. Mintle suggests this approach: "If a trusted woman confirms that your weight is a good issue to work on, use this information as a wake-up call to get healthy and take care of yourself."

Remember that, as we said in the chapter, this conversation is primarily about ways we can take better care of ourselves, and we are only dealing with weight, fitness, and appearance issues that we can do something about in a positive way. If you find that you are tempted to starve yourself, purge, or do anything else that might hurt your body as a result of what you read here, you have misunderstood, and we beg you to talk to a trusted adult immediately.

Even if you realize you do want to work on a more healthy appearance, it's important to remember that God created you to be a special and unique person. When a girl celebrates her God-given individuality, her confidence shines through in a way guys find truly attractive.

> The effort to look nice goes a long way, but there is a balance. I'd rather spend the time with my girlfriend than enjoy the results of the two hours she spent fixing her hair. But that said, yes, it really is nice to see she's put some effort in for me.
> —teen guy quoted in FYWO, pp. 130–31

Rethink

This chapter centered on two main points about guys: (1) guys want "regular" girls with all their individuality, and (2) guys have difficulty being attracted to a girl who doesn't seem to care about taking care of herself. Which of these two points most caught your attention and why?

What, if anything, in this chapter gave you fresh encouragement for having a healthy relationship with a guy? Why?

Is it legitimate that guys say they have difficulty being attracted to a girl who doesn't seem to be making an effort to look good? Does that seem superficial or unfair? Why or why not?

What God-given differences do you see between guys and girls in this area, and what does that mean for us as girls?

Psalm 139:13–14 says, "For you created my inmost being; you knit me together in my mother's womb. I praise you because I am fearfully and wonderfully made; your works are wonderful, I know that full well." How do you feel when you think of yourself as one of God's wonderful creations, designed by the Artist of all life?

React

His Perspective: "Girls have to remember: we don't want a girl we can break. We like your individuality. Throw away your magazines, turn off the TV, and focus just on being healthy." —quote from a teenage guy

Her Response: "I'm one of those girls who is always wondering why I can't get a 'spiritual' guy interested in me. Your book makes it pretty clear that it's because I don't take very good care of myself, especially weight-wise. It's a family problem from way back, believe me, but now I see that I'm really going to have to put some effort in that direction. They say that the definition of insanity is doing all the things you were doing before but expecting a different result. Hello! Thanks for your honesty and for a kick in my size 16 pants!" —e-mail from a teenage girl

Your Insights: How do comments like those above make you feel? Should guys just get over their concern about looks? Should girls feel any responsibility when it comes to their appearance, and why? How does it affect your perspective to realize that guys appreciate individuality and want a real girl, not necessarily a supermodel?

Reconsider
The biggest challenge I face in feeling confident about my appearance is this:

Here's what's changed in my perspective through reading this chapter, and the step I plan to take:

Reflections, Remembrances, and Random Thoughts

Here's what's on my mind this week, Father...

This is the day the LORD has made; let us rejoice and be glad in it.
—Psalm 118:24

Nine out of ten guys say they are attracted to all different types of girls! Only a small minority insists upon the *Sports Illustrated* babe with the perfect body. And that number almost vanished among Christian guys who regularly attend church.

—FYWO, pp. 121–22

To Think About

Why is it hard to believe that all guys aren't interested only in physically gorgeous girls?

Prayer for Today

I know that you look on the heart and commend me for being spiritually pleasing, but help me also to keep my body in good shape as well, as a gift to you and to my future husband.

Girls who are "over the top" are out. Too much makeup, fake tan, fake nails, and fake hair is a turnoff. Makes me think they're hung up on themselves and wouldn't give the relationship a chance.

—teen guy quoted in FYWO, p. 139

To Think About

What signals might I be sending out that say I'm either hung up on outward appearances or don't care about my appearance at all?

Prayer for Today

Father, in a world of pretense, teach me to be real. Help me trust you for the right guy who will love me just the way I am. Thank you that you love me that way!

To Think About

What are my God-given strengths—the reasons I can walk confidently as his precious daughter?

I do not feel obliged to believe that the same God who has endowed us with sense, reason, and intellect has intended us to forgo their use.

—Galileo Galilei

Prayer for Today

Father, protect me from the temptation to think I'm not pretty enough or good enough. Help me to remember that you created me and you're shaping me into a woman after your own heart.

An average girl is more beautiful, I think. She's more real, and accessible. I can't explain it, but it's like "the girl next door" is someone I can have a conversation with...versus an untouchable debutante.

—teen guy quoted in FYWO, p. 123

To Think About

Am I confident in who I am? Do I believe that I'm a person others enjoy spending time with?

Prayer for Today

Father, help me to receive your perspective on what makes me truly beautiful. Even as I honor you by taking care of my body, your temple, help me to remember that what's in my heart matters even more.

Sometimes I look at a girl and try to picture her doing the things I dream about doing some day... like spending time on the mission field, working in an orphanage. If I can't picture it, I'm not going to date her.

—teen guy quoted in FYWO, p. 124

To Think About

What kind of effort could I make, along with God's help, to mold my body into a temple of the Holy Spirit?

Charm is deceptive, and beauty is fleeting; but a woman who fears the LORD is to be praised.
—Proverbs 31:30

God's Answers to Prayer This Week

Pray not to be seen of men but to be heard of God.

—John Mason

Report on Last Week's Real-Life Challenge

These are some of the images I noticed in the media and throughout my daily routine that might be eye-magnet problems for guys:

_____
_____
_____
_____
_____
_____
_____

When I looked for examples of females who could dress attractively without the "lure," here's what I noticed:

_____
_____
_____
_____
_____
_____

As I evaluated my wardrobe and attitudes, I realized I could help the guys I care about by making the following changes:

1 _____
_____

2 _____
_____

3 _____
_____

Relate—Inner and Outer Beauty

Talk with your trusted friends, and compare notes on what you learned this week. Look back through your journal entries from this week, and write here a few things you'd like to discuss regarding guys' perspectives on outward appearances or other things you learned about health and body image.

You may want to discuss the following questions with your friends:

- What were your thoughts about the questions on pages 123–24?
- Do you think it's inconsistent for guys to say they want realness in girls and yet say they want girls they can be physically attracted to? If not, what is consistent about it?
- What evidence have you seen to confirm or disprove the survey results that nine out of ten guys say they are attracted to all types of girls, including the unglamorous or stocky girls?
- What can we realistically do to be sure we look our best—without becoming overly obsessed with outward appearances?

Rewind and Replay

Angela's feelings for Lance had started in high school when she felt insecure about her looks. At that time, the grapevine gossip that Lance was interested in her seemed too hard to believe, so she hadn't sent any encouraging signals. And anyway, she'd been busy playing on the softball team, where her stockier, more powerful figure was an asset.

But now that they were two years out of high school, things were different. She felt more comfortable in her own skin, and their friendship had grown into the serious romance she'd dreamed of. Lance obviously enjoyed their time together, which fed her confidence.

They soon fell into the pattern of going to his favorite ice-cream parlor every Friday night and ordering double scoops of the weekly special. Angela loved these quiet moments when she and Lance talked deeply about their lives. She sometimes ordered a second round of ice cream just so they could linger. Sure, she was putting on a few pounds—especially since she no longer played softball— but she wasn't about to give up these precious nights. Besides, Lance wouldn't be so shallow as to judge her on appearances.

But lately he seemed less affectionate. And instead of taking her to their special place each Friday, Lance often suggested going to a coffee shop or taking a walk in the park. And when they did go to the ice-cream place, he ordered only a single scoop with no toppings and seemed embarrassed when she ordered a double. Around others, he was pleasant enough, but he didn't seem proud to introduce her as his date. What was up with that? Was he slipping away? Maybe she just needed to draw him in closer and let him know how much she really cared.

1. What was Angela's primary assumption about how Lance felt about her looks in high school? What is her assumption about his view of her appearance now?

2. Put yourself in Lance's shoes. What might have initially attracted him to Angela?
3. What do you think prompted the change in Lance's attitude toward Angela? Was this shift justified? Why or why not?
4. What mistake, if any, had Angela made in her evaluation of their relationship?
5. When she sensed Lance's distance, what did Angela decide to do? Was that a good response? Why or why not?
6. If you were in Angela's place, what solution would you try for strengthening your relationship with Lance?

Note: After you think over these questions, check out the Inside His Head section at the end of this book to see what Lance was actually thinking.

Real-Life Challenge

Here are some action challenges for you this week:

- Take some time this week to evaluate where you're doing well in taking care of yourself and letting your inner confidence shine through your outer appearance. Also try to identify any blind spots in this area.
- Would you be brave enough to ask an adult woman, female friend, or doctor to be honest with you about realistic areas you might improve upon? In other words, *not* the out-of-reach fantasy ideals of the magazines. (Note: Please do not ask a guy, especially not your father. No guy wants to be put in the position of possibly hurting the feelings of a girl he cares about.)

You can jot down notes about the outcome of this challenge on page 164 and, if you feel comfortable doing so, share your answers with the group next time you meet.

BODY LANGUAGE

His Physical Desires Mean Emotional
Consequences for Both of You

Recap
Teenage guys are conflicted by their powerful physical urges, which also have massive emotional consequences, and they need you to help protect both of you.

When it comes to going too far sexually, many guys feel neither the ability nor the responsibility to draw the line and stop. And those who do feel a sense of responsibility in this area don't want to have to stop it alone. They want and need girls' help to set boundaries and avoid giving in to the overwhelming temptations of the moment.

In general, Christian guys feel a much higher degree of responsibility in the area of sex and have a greater knowledge of the dynamics and repercussions of sexual involvement, but they, too, are asking for girls' help in resisting temptation.

Two-thirds of guys confirmed that having sex with a girl does not equal significant commitment to her. Although the guys admit they're usually the ones pressing for sex, two out of three said that they doubted they could ever trust a girl again after she gave in to their request for sex. Even more guys of all religious beliefs—and nearly ninety percent of Christian guys—say they want to marry a virgin.

Many guys were surprisingly romantic in their responses to the topic of a girl's virginity, declaring their desire to be heroes to girls, not heartbreaking hindrances. They emphasized that while they hoped their future bride would wait, they placed greatest importance on her purity of heart, even if she'd made past mistakes.

> Don't go around selling yourself just because
> that is what you think you should be doing.
> The right guy will come eventually.
> —teen guy quoted in FYWO, p. 171

Rethink

What was the most important thing you learned about guys from this chapter?

What's generally on the minds of girls when they give in to sexual temptation? How is this different from what guys are usually thinking when it comes to having sex?

Is it fair that many guys expect girls to set the boundaries? Why or why not? How much does "fair" matter when it comes to drawing the line?

How does it make you feel to hear that many guys are looking for purity over perfection and that they want to be heroes to girls? Does this sound old-fashioned and outdated, or do you find it encouraging? Explain your answer.

As you think about the man you hope to marry, what do you wish you could say to any girls he may date before you meet him? What do you think he'd like you to know?

Philippians 4:8 says, "Whatever is true, whatever is noble, whatever is right, whatever is pure, whatever is lovely, whatever is admirable—if anything is excellent or praiseworthy—think about such things." In what ways might you avoid future heartache by deliberately focusing your thoughts now?

React

His Perspective: "With sex, it's almost like buyer's remorse. We see this beautiful thing and think our lives will be better when we get that shiny toy. But like a toy, soon you see you've tarnished it, and it will never be the same thrill. You're wondering if that decision was such a great idea in the first place. There are doubts that come immediately. Are there going to be attachments and hurt feelings? There are suddenly expectations and emotions that go well beyond a physical act. You've bonded yourself to another human, and you're suddenly responsible for her for a long time. The carefree thing is totally gone. You can't look at her again if you break up. If you are a lady of strong moral character, I ask, on behalf of all guys, that you restate your position—kindly—once in a while and help us stay out of situations and places that could be compromising and regret-filled." —quote from a guy-on-the-street interview

Her Response: "I'm one of those girls who made the life-altering mistake of having premarital sex, and I've regretted it every day since. I'm glad there are guys out there who understand temptation and mistakes and are forgiving and looking at the heart instead of the history. I'm grateful for God's grace and for guys who want to be girls' heroes." —comment from a seventeen-year-old girl who lost her virginity at fifteen

Your Insights: Do you think girls also feel "buyer's remorse" after sexual boundaries have been violated? Why or why not? What new insights did you gain from this chapter, and how will those insights affect your future interactions with guys?

Reconsider

Here's what I never before realized about how guys approach the issue of sex and boundaries:

Now that I know this, here's how it will affect my decisions from here on:

Reflections, Remembrances, and Random Thoughts

Here's what's on my mind this week, Father...

*Be anxious for nothing, but in everything by
prayer and supplication, with thanksgiving,
let your requests be made known to God.*
—Philippians 4:6 (NKJV)

With basic making out, it's usually innocent for me. But once the hands start moving, it leads to more stuff. I can usually restrain myself if the girl isn't pushing things too much, but if she is...

—teen guy quoted in FYWO, p. 148

Okay, this might sound bad, but I have a message for the teenage girls out there: When it comes to sex, don't trust us. We aren't in our right minds. Stay out of that situation!

—quote from a guy-on-the-street interview

To Think About

What personal rules should I put in place now so that I don't slip and do something I'll regret later?

Prayer for Today

Father, I ask for your gift of self-control when I'm with a guy. Your Word says I have this quality in my character because I have your Holy Spirit, and I ask that you would give me the strength to use it well when I'm in a tempting situation. I trust you.

If you find yourself in a place of strong temptation, we urge you to "do a Joseph," and run! Help your guy protect both of you from hurting each other, your relationship, your future, and your relationship with God.

—FYWO, p. 169

To Think About

As I think back on past temptations—of any kind—what has been the consequence of not running?

Prayer for Today

Thank you, Lord, that you've promised to provide a way of escape from any temptation. Give me the courage to flee from sexual immorality.

To Think About

What do I think the guys
I know would say about
my reputation?

A good name is more desirable than great riches.

—Proverbs 22:1

Prayer for Today

Father, I ask you to give me wisdom and self-control, so that my actions will honor you in every way.

Be careful. It's okay to fall in love, but remember that guys usually have other intentions than falling in love. It's very easy to be taken advantage of in today's world. It may not seem like a big deal now to be physical with numerous guys, but you will regret it when you are ready to move on with your life and start a family.

—teen guy quoted in FYWO, p. 154

To Think About

Am I doing anything that puts my heart—or my reputation—at risk?

Prayer for Today

Lord, please don't let me be deceived. Remind me of what true love looks like, and help me recognize and resist the counterfeit.

I love it best when she just puts her head on my shoulder. Feeling her hair on the back of my neck is so great; it's all I need right now. I want to maintain the innocence of this level.

—teen guy quoted in FYWO, p. 170

To Think About

What are some ways
I can demonstrate the
depth of my feelings
without sacrificing
innocence?

*Flee the evil desires of youth, and pursue righteousness,
faith, love and peace, along with those who call
on the Lord out of a pure heart.*
—2 Timothy 2:22

God's Answers to Prayer This Week

You should, with
a holy conspiracy,
besiege heaven.

—Tertullian

Report on Last Week's Real-Life Challenge

Here are some things I'm confident I'm doing right when it comes to caring for myself:

1 _____

2 _____

3 _____

Here's one area where I think making some changes might help me feel better about myself:

_____

Relate—Body Language

If you feel comfortable doing so, talk with your trusted friends, and compare notes on what you learned this week. Look back through your journal entries from this week and write here a few things you'd like to discuss regarding sexual issues and setting boundaries with guys.

The following questions may help get the conversation going:
- What were your thoughts about the questions on pages 146–48?
- Were you surprised to read that two-thirds of guys said that having sex with a girl does not equal a significant commitment to that girl? How is this different from what many girls believe?
- What lies do girls tend to tell themselves when they're feeling internal or external pressure to have sex?
- What steps can we take to help a guy hold back his strong sex drive?

Rewind and Replay

Courtney loved college. And she really loved dating frat guys—especially that cutie Blake. On weekends, he was always up for a party with friends to shake off the stress of a tough week of classes. Afterward, Courtney would often come up to his room where they'd sit on the bed and talk—and, if his roommate wasn't there, make out. Once, his roommate walked in on them. As he laughed and retreated into the hall, Courtney heard him yell, "Hey, guys! Maybe Blake's finally gonna get some tonight!" Blake looked questioningly at her. She tried to cover her discomfort with a teasing comeback: "Not tonight, you're not!"

But as things progressed, Courtney realized she was falling head over heels for this guy. When they started saying, "I love you," to each other, it became increasingly difficult to hold off sex. One night, she didn't want to stop.

Having crossed the line once, there seemed little reason to hold back. Soon she and Blake were having sex any time her roommate or his was away. It was fun and exciting, but as the months passed, something in their relationship was changing. Was it her imagination or was Blake weirding out on her, sometimes acting all lovey-dovey but other times being distant and even cruel?

And what was the deal with Bethany, that girl she'd caught him talking with several times? Wasn't she the one the guys said wouldn't put out? What could Blake possibly see in her? Courtney was scared she was losing him. She had his body; now she'd just have to work a little harder at reeling in his heart.

1. What were the main factors that led Courtney to cross the line into having sex?
2. Which of these factors were brought about by her own choices? What could she have done to bring about a different outcome?

3. Put yourself in Blake's shoes. List some of the reasons he might want to have sex with Courtney.
4. Keep yourself in his shoes. Once they did have sex, why did Blake start "weirding out"? What might have changed in his perspective of her?
5. How would you answer Courtney's question about what Blake could possibly see in Bethany?
6. What's the wisest thing Courtney could do at this point?

Note: After you think over these questions, check out the Inside His Head section at the end of this book to see what Blake was actually thinking.

Real-Life Challenge

Here are some action challenges for you this week:

- Think about your personal dating rules. What specific physical boundaries have you set that you're determined never to cross before marriage? For example, maybe you've decided it's okay to kiss a guy while standing by the front door, but not alone in the car or in a room with the door closed. Now that you know how guys think, where do you need to set firmer or stricter boundaries?
- If you're currently in a dating relationship, discuss these boundaries with your boyfriend and put them to work. If you're not currently in a dating relationship, how will you put these boundaries into practice when you are in one?

You can jot down notes about the outcome of this challenge on page 188.

WORDS FOR YOUR HEART

What Guys *Really* Want to Tell You

Recap

At the end of the survey, when the guys were asked about the best advice they'd like to give teen girls, the most common answer by far was something like this: "Be yourself, because you are more valuable than you think."

One of the most gratifying discoveries of our research process came when we offered guys the opportunity to speak straight from the heart, expressing in their own words what they most wish girls could know. Over and over, guys said they want to encourage us girls to have a strong understanding of our value and to break free from the pressure to be someone we aren't. They also said that they wanted us to stand firm and not compromise things that are important (especially, as many of them mentioned, when it comes to sex).

The same guys who admitted their struggle with trusting girls, lusting over cute bodies, and pushing limits in the sexual arena freely offered the beautiful advice every girl wants and needs to hear:

Be confident. Be yourself. And never compromise.

 Honestly, I would teach girls to be confident. Girls are still brought up seeing tall lanky supermodels being called

beautiful, and they believe that if they don't look the same way they're ugly. Women need to be more confident, whether that is confidence in their appearance or even in their ability to talk to a guy. A girl who knows what she wants and isn't afraid to show it is the most appealing girl of all.
—teen guy quoted in FYWO, p. 179

Rethink

What comment in this chapter meant the most to you, and why?

How has your view of guys changed, if it has, as you've read *For Young Women Only?*

What findings or comments from guys have really stayed with you?

How has your view of yourself changed as you've read *For Young Women Only*?

Have you made any new commitments as you've read through the book and engaged more deeply with the material through this journal? What are the two or three top things you would like to commit to work on in the weeks and months to come?

1

2

3

Philippians 1:6 says, "He [God] who began a good work in you will carry it on to completion until the day of Christ Jesus." Describe the ways that God is working in your life right now.

_____

_____

_____

_____

_____

_____

_____

React

His Perspective: "Confidence is one of the most attractive things a girl can have. Even average-looking girls, if they'll hold their head high and boldly tell a joke, or goof around with a guy, it's so attractive. Girls who know who they are and where they're going are great catches, and guys know this." —quote from a guy-on-the-street interview

Her Response: "This chapter got me thinking: I know that guys love confidence, but when I'm confident I'm actually exposing a side of me that can be easily shot down. It feels vulnerable to be confident and put myself out there. The other side of it that I've seen, though, is that guys don't judge girls on how much we're liked, but how cool we are if we're not liked or if we're put down. It's how I react to the bad, not the good. That's where character shines—in bad situations. If you respond well, even if guys rejected you before, they see how you buck up under pressure and realize that maybe they missed out on something good." —e-mail from a seventeen-year-old girl

Your Insights: In what circumstances does your confidence shine through? Do you often find yourself trying to please others, or are you sure of where you stand with your own values and life direction? In areas where you aren't sure of yourself or feel doubtful about how to stand firm, what can you do to build your confidence?

Reconsider
As I read about all these guys encouraging girls to "be yourself," I realized:

One change I plan to make is...

Reflections, Remembrances, and Random Thoughts

Here's what's on my mind this week, Father...

Cast all your anxiety on him because he cares for you.
—1 Peter 5:7

Besides "wear sun-screen" and "tip well," my advice to teen girls is, "understand your identity." You are a valuable creation of God with an awesome future ahead of you.

—teen guy quoted in FYWO, p. 116

To Think About

What kind of future is God preparing me for?

Prayer for Today

Lord, would you set me apart and seal me for your purposes? Would you protect me from the Enemy's plans and help me to hit the bull's-eye of the target you are launching me toward?

Don't be afraid to be yourself. If they don't like you for you, then they aren't worth your time.

—teen guy quoted in FYWO, p. 176

No one can make you feel inferior without your consent.

—Eleanor Roosevelt

To Think About

In what circumstances and around which people am I tempted to hide my true self? Why do I feel that way?

Prayer for Today

Lord, I know that my future holds happiness and trials, joys and frustrations, love and dislike, loyalty and betrayal. I pray that no matter what circumstances come my way, I would please you by my godly responses.

To Think About

If I could wave a magic wand and change one thing about myself, what would it be?

With God all things
are possible.

—Matthew 19:26

Prayer for Today

*Father, I trust you with the deepest desires of my heart.
Thank you for listening to and caring about my hopes, and please
show me where my dreams might conflict with your marvelous plans.*

There are only two ways to live your life. One is as though nothing is a miracle. The other is as though everything is a miracle.

—Albert Einstein

To Think About

What amazing blessings are present in my life right now?

Prayer for Today

Lord, I praise you for the countless ways you show your love to me every day. Help me to slow down and appreciate the miracle of every moment.

I dare you to live. Don't look back and look on all the opportunities where you didn't step out. Live from your heart.

—teen guy quoted in FYWO, p. 180

To Think About

If I had no fear, what would I do differently today?

For God has not given us a spirit of fear, but of power and of love and of a sound mind.
—2 Timothy 1:7 (NKJV)

God's Answers to Prayer This Week

I will praise the
LORD at all times.

—Psalm 34:1 (NLT)

Report on Last Week's Real-Life Challenge

As I considered what I learned from chapter 7, I realized I needed to strengthen my boundaries in a few areas:

These are the specific boundaries I've set for myself:

1.

2.

3.

This is how I plan to be true to these boundaries in my current relationship or in a future relationship:

Relate—Words for Your Heart

Talk with your trusted friends about the encouraging words you read from the guys this week, and talk about what advice you found most helpful. Look back through your journal entries from this week, and write here anything you'd like to discuss. Also include some words of encouragement to share with them.

As you connect with your friends, consider sharing your answers to the following questions:

- What were your thoughts about the questions on pages 170–72?
- Is it harder for girls to be true to themselves around other girls or around guys? Why?
- What aspects of your character would you like to continue to develop, such as confidence, encouraging words, or a listening ear? What aspects would you like to leave behind?
- What is the most important thing you've learned about guys from this book?

Real-Life Challenge

You can work through this challenge now, either with your friends or on your own, or you can give it some thought in the days ahead. Either way, use the space provided to write down some thoughts. Then refer back to them when you need a boost.

Consider the people around you who exude confidence without being fake or proud. What effect does their presence have on others?

You may want to recruit help from a trusted friend for this one. Think through all things that make you a unique person, the characteristics and strengths that define you. Then make a list for those days when you could use a reminder that you are truly valuable.

1

2

3

4

5

6

7

8

9

10

Appendix

INSIDE HIS HEAD

Looking at the Rewind and Replay Case Studies from the Guy's Point of View

Warning! Don't read these until you've worked through the case studies using the new insights you've gained. Of course, if you're completely stumped about the guy's thinking, you can peek back here for some help.

Chapter Two

Greg had been looking forward to the youth-group ski trip for weeks. Since his girlfriend Allison would be skiing for the first time, he'd been making plans to show his beautiful beginner the ropes. Even though his family didn't have much money, he'd found a way to pursue his passion for skiing by carefully saving up from his summer jobs.

On the bus ride up, Greg sat with Allison and gave her a few tips he had learned over the years—tips that had been helpful to others who tried them. As he saw her excitement and even her nervousness, he could hardly wait to get there. He pictured himself protectively guiding her down the slopes, encouraging her to go for it or helping her up after a fall.

When they arrived, he was horrified to see Allison veer off and sign up for individual lessons—with a college ski instructor, no less! Greg tried to keep his face blank as his gut twisted. Why didn't Allison trust *him* to teach her how to ski? Did she think he'd been exaggerating his experience or something? If Allison couldn't trust him to teach her his best sport, what did she really think about him? And why was she flaunting her family's money with the new skis and lessons? Was she trying to say he wasn't good enough? Greg turned toward the ski lift with his buddy, mortified that one of his friends had witnessed his humiliation.

Chapter Three

Tyler was thrilled to see a beautiful girl bouncing a ball at the neighborhood basketball court. He promptly challenged her to a game of one-on-one—after stealing the ball and launching it toward the basket. For a frozen moment he worried that it wouldn't go in and he'd look like a fool, but it was a perfect shot.

When Hannah started trash talking right back, Tyler was delighted. This was his kind of girl! But delight turned to embarrassment as she scored repeatedly. Sure, he wasn't the best basketball player around—he'd known better than to try out for the team—but he didn't think he was this terrible. He was relieved to be able to use the excuse of dinner to take off and avoid any more humiliation.

The next day, Tyler ran into a buddy who mentioned that the new girl was expected to be the star of the JV basketball team. So he felt better. A little. She *was* pretty cute…maybe he'd ask her out if no one else got to her first.

When Hannah walked into algebra class Monday morning, he decided to let the other guys know he had first dibs by mentioning that they'd shot hoops together. But before he could finish his sentence, Hannah challenged, "Tell 'em who smoked who!" Despite the humiliation burning in his stomach, Tyler laughed along with the rest of the class and even cracked a joke to cover the fact that he felt like a complete idiot and a miserable basketball player. It would be a long time before he played with Hannah again.

Chapter Four

Rick loved mixing it up in football, but he'd learned the hard way to be careful off the field. Being physically battered was one thing, but he wasn't into getting heart damage from people he wasn't sure he could trust.

One of those people was Jen. She was hot, no question. He'd angled to sit next to her when the gang went out for pizza, and he'd scored the privilege of driving her home a few times. But she wouldn't stop ragging on him about his old car. Rick laughed it off at first, but her teasing quickly grew annoying. She seemed to think it was hilarious to give him a hard time about every little thing.

Still, he got a kick from the jealous looks of other guys when he sat next to her or walked with her in the hallway. But he quickly learned she wasn't someone he could trust with any secrets. When he heard Jen gossiping about Suzy at the Friday night pizza gathering, he started to wonder whether Jen's physical qualities really made up for the rest. Suzy was one of the nicest girls in school, and Rick had never heard her gossip about anyone. In fact, he knew Suzy had spotted that D he'd gotten on a recent paper, but as far as he knew, she hadn't told a soul. Jen would probably have broadcast it to the whole school within five minutes.

So what if Suzy wasn't the most popular girl around? She was caring and unselfish, and when she made a joke, it wasn't at someone else's expense. Maybe it was time to stop going after Jen and find a girl who was more trustworthy.

Chapter Five

James had always enjoyed Vicki as a friend, and he secretly hoped she might become something more down the road. For years they'd enjoyed swimming together each summer and goofing off with friends at the lake. But this year, Vicki had suddenly developed a figure, and she was attracting a lot of attention—especially when she wore her bikini. The sexy photo she'd posted on MySpace sure didn't make it easy for him when they chatted online each night.

Not that James didn't like pretty girls—just the opposite. He had a really, really tough time not looking! The youth pastor was always challenging the guys to flee temptation and "take every thought captive," but how could he, with Vicki constantly flaunting her body? Whenever she came out of the water in that little bikini, a movie played in his head of what it would look like if that bikini wasn't there. Furious with himself, he'd look away and try to blank out those thoughts.

He wanted to honor God—and Vicki. But then he'd catch sight of her romping on the lakeshore and suddenly have an image of her romping with him—in bed. Frustrated, James realized the only solution was to limit his time with her. That made him mad, because he liked going to the lake. But he knew he couldn't trust himself, and he was starting to wonder whether he could trust Vicki. Didn't she know what she was doing to him and all the other guys in the vicinity? She seemed to be turning into the kind of girl who tempted guys to dishonor the values that were important to them. If so, he thought sadly, it was time to back away.

Chapter Six

Lance had wanted to date Angela for years, and when he finally got his chance after high school, he was both thrilled and proud. What guy wouldn't want gorgeous, personality-plus Angela on his arm? Sure, she didn't look like the bimbo models on TV, but who wanted that anyway? He liked her curves and loved that she liked the active life as much as he did. He also enjoyed their Friday night tradition of talking at his favorite ice-cream parlor.

For a while, that is. After a few months of their ice-cream tradition, he noticed that her clothes seemed to be fitting tighter. *No biggie*, he thought. *She'll just work out a bit more, cut back, and take the extra pounds off. After all, she's always taken great care of herself.* But as the weeks passed, she started eating *more* ice cream, not less! And he couldn't remember the last time she had wanted to do something active.

Lance started feeling a strange sense of panic inside. He'd been thinking of popping the question, but if Angela let herself go like this even before marriage, what on earth would it be like afterward? He'd watched two of his buddies marry adorable girls who seemed to stop caring about their appearance soon after the wedding. Yes, the guys still loved their wives, but they definitely weren't happy. Their wives didn't seem to get how important it was to their men that they take care of themselves.

And now he was seeing those signs even *before* he and Angela got married! He longed for the energetic girl she'd been in high school, but now he felt like he was dating her frumpy aunt! Worst of all, Angela was getting clingy. Had she quit worrying about her looks because she thought she "owned" him? How could he possibly let on that he wished she would make an effort to regain her healthy, attractive figure and active lifestyle?

Chapter Seven

Blake's parents had been super strict while he was living at home, and now that he was eighteen, he was ready to get out and par-tay! His first order of business at university was to land a great girl, and Courtney seemed perfect. She was tall, shapely, fun at a party, and *really* fun after the party!

As his makeout sessions with Courtney got hotter and heavier, Blake knew this was the girl who would finally relieve him of his virginity. He'd been cringing for months as his frat brothers teased him about his innocent status. So he was walking tall when he and Courtney finally crossed the line.

As the months passed, however, a weird sense of guilt and distrust started to really bug him. He was thrilled they were having sex, but he couldn't help wondering why Courtney had given in so quickly. They hadn't really known each other that long. What had she done with other guys in the past? More critically, what might she do with other guys in the future?

Blake felt schizophrenic. He piled on the charm when he wanted Courtney, but the next day he'd have crazy thoughts about not trusting her. Suspicion whispered in his head, "I'll bet she's going to do the same thing with another guy…"

By contrast, he found himself enjoying more and more his uncomplicated interactions with that sweet girl he'd met in biology. He'd heard that Bethany was a virgin with serious boundaries, yet he felt jealous when he learned his roommate planned to ask her out. What was wrong with him? He'd gotten what he wanted with Courtney, but now their relationship seemed burdened with guilt—and he resented it. After all, she could have said no, couldn't she? It was just as much her fault as his.

Maybe it was time to make a fresh start—with another girl.

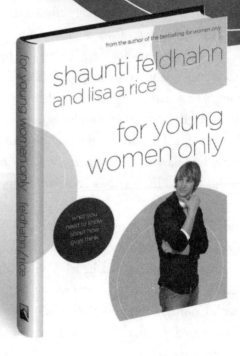